KU-845-346

GREAT ARTISTS COLLECTION

Five centuries of great art in full colour

GOYA

by ENRIQUETA HARRIS

ENCYCLOPAEDIA BRITANNICA : LONDON

Volume six

COVER: Detail from the *Portrait of Antonia Zárate* (*Plate 25*)

© *1969 by Phaidon Press Limited, London*

This revised edition published in 1972
by Encyclopaedia Britannica International Limited, London

ISBN 0 85229 106 X

Printed in Great Britain

GOYA

The greatness of Goya is more widely acknowledged today than ever before. As a portrait painter, as a creator of menacing and melancholy images in oils, as a master of enigmatic, satirical and revolutionary drawing and engraving, as the champion of the Spanish people in their struggle against oppression, and the recorder of their life and customs and their sufferings in war, he is known and appreciated everywhere. Today every major collection in the world possesses some of his engravings, which were published in successive editions from Goya's own plates, the most recent being issued in 1937, during the Spanish Civil War. The two hundred and ninety-two engravings are, of course, the most portable and therefore, in the physical sense, the most accessible of Goya's works. To judge his achievement as a painter, however, one must still go to Spain itself. Most of the chief galleries of Europe and the Americas contain, to be sure, examples of his painting, and some of these represent him at his best and most characteristic. But of approximately five hundred works with any title to authenticity, nearly a third are in Madrid and almost half are preserved in Spain. No gallery outside Spain possesses more than a dozen.

Though Goya was in his lifetime the foremost painter in Spain, his fame in this medium did not extend to the rest of Europe. His only foreign patrons appear to have been the Duke of Wellington and the few Frenchmen who sat to him for their portraits – and most of these portraits were painted in Spain. He was little known abroad except as the author of the *Caprichos*. Even in Spain his reputation was in eclipse before he died. In 1828, the year of Goya's death, the catalogue of the Prado Museum in Madrid, for which he himself had provided the brief autobiographical notice, contained only three of his canvases. Today the Prado possesses some one hundred and eighteen pictures. He had little or no immediate influence in his own country and when he retired at the age of eighty as First Court Painter he was succeeded, not by a pupil or follower, but by an exponent of the neo-classical style, Vicente López. His move to France in the last years of his life did not, apparently, make him better known abroad. The first signs of Goya's European reputation came after his death, among the new generation of French Romantics, who were admirers, in particular, of the *Caprichos*. One of the earliest of these was Delacroix, who made copies of some of them. It was to him that the first monograph on Goya, published in Paris by Laurent Matheron, was dedicated in 1858. Before Matheron, writers such as Théophile Gautier and Baudelaire had done much to make Goya's name known as a painter as well as an engraver and the growth of *hispanisme* at that time, together with the publication in the 1860s of the *Desastres de la Guerra* and the *Proverbios*, combined to make his influence more widespread. The generations of artists who succeeded Delacroix reflect a growing admiration for the Spanish master: from Courbet to Manet and on to Picasso his presence is strongly felt. Their respect for Goya's achievement contributes as much as anything to his reputation as the forerunner of so many movements in European painting of the 19th and 20th centuries.

It is naturally for the revolutionary character of his art that Goya, the great Spanish old master, earned the title of 'first of the moderns'. But his originality can only be fully appreciated if it is seen in relation to his position as an 'official' artist and to his conventional professional career. For during most of his life – for fifty-three of his eighty-two years – Goya was a servant of the Spanish Crown and for nearly thirty years First Court Painter to three successive Spanish Kings. Elected to the Royal Academy of San Fernando at the age of thirty-four, in 1780, he was for several years its Deputy Director and Director of Painting, with teaching duties. By far the majority of his paintings are the result of official commissions: tapestry cartoons, portraits and religious subjects. It is his official works and the public honours that he won that take pride of place in Goya's early Spanish biographies, by his son and his friend Valentín Carderera. In his version Carderera also gives a hint of the rebellious character that legend later attributed to the painter, on the evidence chiefly of his art: 'If Goya had written his life it would perhaps have afforded as much interest as that of Benvenuto Cellini'.

Modern investigations of his 'unofficial' works, particularly the graphic art, have thrown much light on Goya's critical attitude to many aspects of the contemporary world. But the mystery that still surrounds much of his life and many of his works is the result of the many gaps in our knowledge. Not enough material for a coherent and comprehensive account is yet available. Only a part of the documents relating to his official career has so far been found and only a selection of his large private correspondence is in print. One of the mysteries that is perhaps too deep ever to be solved is that first propounded by Matheron, more than a hundred years ago: 'Comme ce diable d'homme devait se trouver à l'étroit dans son costume de peintre du roi.'

Francisco José Goya y Lucientes was born on 30 March, 1746, at Fuendetodos, an Aragonese village near Saragossa, and died at Bordeaux on 16 April, 1828. The first half of his life was spent under the peaceful and relatively enlightened rule of Charles III. The second half was lived in a turbulent atmosphere of political and social unrest, which reflected and was created by the events in France that led to and followed the Revolution, in a period of foreign invasion and civil war, succeeded by a wave of reaction that led Goya eventually to seek voluntary exile in France. Goya's enormous output of paintings, drawings and engravings, produced during a working life of more than sixty years' passionate activity, record innumerable aspects of the life of his contemporaries and of the changing world in which he lived. It also reflects the personal crises which were the result of illness, in particular that which left him permanently and totally deaf at the age of forty-seven.

Not much is known of Goya's early life as a painter but it seems to have followed a conventional pattern. The son of a master gilder, he began his studies in Saragossa, at the age of thirteen, with a local artist, José Luzán, who had trained in Naples and who taught him to draw, to copy engravings and to paint in oils. In 1763 and 1766 he competed unsuccessfully for scholarships offered by the Royal Academy of San Fernando in Madrid, probably working during this time in the studio of the court painter Francisco Bayeu (Pl. 8), a fellow townsman whose sister Goya married in 1773. Unable to gain support for a journey to Italy, he went to Rome on his own account, according to his son, to continue his studies. Goya himself later asserted that he had lived there at his own expense, presumably by his brush. His meeting with the painter Jacques-Louis David, which Matheron reports Goya as having spoken of in his old age, is problematical; David was not in Italy at the time and there is no evidence that the two great contemporary artists ever met. All that is known for certain of Goya's Italian sojourn is that in April 1771 he was in Rome and from there submitted a painting to a competition held by the Academy in Parma, which had been announced in the previous year. He described himself as a Roman and a pupil of Bayeu. Goya's entry, which has not survived, had for its subject Hannibal's first sight of Italy from the Alps. It won six votes and the comment that 'if his colours had been truer to nature and his composition closer to the subject it would have created doubts about the winner of the prize'. The winner was Paolo Borroni, a painter of little note today. It is not known how long Goya was in Italy. All we have to go on is his son's statement that his affection for his parents made him cut short his stay and the knowledge that by the end of 1771 he was back in Saragossa and receiving his first official commission, for frescoes in the Cathedral of El Pilar. Since there are no paintings that can be dated with certainty before 1771, it is difficult to determine what Goya learned from his visit to Italy. It is possible that he acquired the technique of fresco painting there, but against that we must set the fact that his first frescoes in Saragossa show the influence of the rococo styles of Italian artists whose works he could have seen without leaving Spain. The Neapolitan Corrado Giaquinto, for example, traces of whose style have been discerned in Goya's early work, had been active in Spain for many years and after his departure the Venetian Giovanni Battista Tiepolo had executed many commissions there. Tiepolo, with his two sons, was employed at the Spanish court from 1762 until his death in 1770. His work was one of the principal formative influences on Goya's earliest known style and it is even possible that Goya met him in Madrid before he went to Italy.

The next important influence came from a very different source, the German artist Anton Raphael Mengs, the friend of Winckelmann and celebrated exponent of neo-classicism. Mengs had gone to Spain as court painter the year before Tiepolo and when he returned there from a visit to Italy in 1773, after Tiepolo's death, he became undisputed art dictator. Indeed, according to his English translator, 'he enjoyed such fame that not to admire him was almost a violence against Church and State'. It is possible that it was in Rome that Goya first met Mengs, since many years later he wrote that it was Mengs who made him return to Spain. In any event, it was Mengs who started him on his career at court by summoning him in 1774 to work, with other young artists, on models for tapestries to be woven at the Royal Factory of Santa Barbara. Under the direction first of Mengs, and later of his brother-in-law, Francisco Bayeu, and Mariano Maella, Goya produced over sixty tapestry cartoons at intervals between 1775 and 1792.

These cartoons are important both from the point of view of the subjects represented and because of the stylistic development to which they bear witness. In the first place, they gave Goya his first opportunity to use those national subjects for which he was later so famous. Until Mengs' time the tapestries woven in Madrid had been based on literary, allegorical and peasant themes after French and Flemish paintings. Goya and his fellow artists were allowed for the first time – subject to the approval of their designs by the King – a much freer hand. Original compositions and new subjects, portraying typically Spanish scenes, now became the vogue, and we find the writer Antonio Ponz, in 1782, commending the recent tapestries based on paintings by Goya and other artists for representing 'the costumes and diversions of the present time'. These scenes of contemporary life, particularly of life in Madrid, illustrations of aristocratic and popular pastimes – *fêtes galantes à l'espagnole* – reflect the new taste for such topics which is also evident in contemporary Spanish literature, especially in the theatre. In painting Goya was to exploit them more than any other Spanish artist of his age.

It is this new subject matter which is singled out by the French Ambassador

Bourgoing, whose *Nouveau Voyage en Espagne* was first published in 1789. Goya is mentioned as one of the painters who helped to recompense the Spaniards for the loss of Mengs and is praised for the 'pleasing style in which he portrays the manners, customs and games of his country'. Mengs, in fact, had left Spain in 1776, but his presence is evident in the early cartoons, where the influence of Tiepolo's decorative style is modified by the teaching and example of the German painter, especially his insistence on simplicity and selective naturalism. In the course of his work on the tapestry cartoons, Goya developed a growing independence of foreign influences and an increasingly individual style, largely inspired by the study of Velázquez – the artist who was for Mengs the greatest exponent of the 'natural style'. About 1778 Goya made a series of sixteen etchings after paintings by Velázquez in the royal collection, which are amongst his earliest engravings. Later in life he acknowledged Velázquez as one of his three masters, the others being Rembrandt and 'above all, nature'. Rembrandt's influence, which must have come almost entirely from his etchings, is certainly visible in Goya's later drawings and engravings, but it was to Velázquez and to nature that his art owed most. Velázquez's example influenced his approach to nature and provided the model for the 'impressionistic' technique that Goya was to develop further than any artist of his age.

Nevertheless, though the later cartoons are in many respects so independent of influence from his contemporaries, they present the same baffling stylistic contradictions as the rest of his work. The cartoons, being well documented, can be dated exactly: on stylistic evidence alone, dating would be more complicated. Even late in this period of growing independence, Goya reverts to an earlier conventional manner and method of composition when the subject seems to demand it. The *Blind Man's Buff* (Pl. 12) and *El Pelele* (Pl. 10), for instance, with their stiffly posed figures with frozen expressions, are altogether less naturalistic than the *Injured Mason* (Pl. 4). The more informal the subject, the more realistically it is portrayed. Nor did Goya always take into consideration the function of the cartoons; the *Blind Guitarist*, one of his own inventions, was returned to him for alteration when the tapestry weavers found it impossible to copy.

It was probably an exaggeration of Goya's son to write that his father's extraordinary facility in painting tapestry cartoons 'astonished' Mengs. Nevertheless, Goya had certainly made an impression on his Director, for when he applied in 1776 for an appointment as Painter to the King (*Pintor del Rey*), he was recommended by Mengs as 'a person of talent and spirit who was likely to make great progress'. This good opinion did not secure Goya the appointment on this occasion or at his next application three years later, after Mengs had left Spain, even though he had the additional support then of Bayeu and Maella. He did not finally obtain the post until 1786. Meanwhile, in 1780, his application for membership of the Royal Academy of San Fernando had been unanimously approved. His admission piece was a *Crucifixion* (Prado), a conventional composition in the manner of Mengs or Bayeu but somewhat influenced by the more naturalistic treatment of Velázquez, whose painting of the same subject he may have known. Shortly afterwards, Goya returned to Saragossa to paint some new frescoes in the Cathedral of El Pilar, a commission which involved him in violent altercation with the authorities and a quarrel with Bayeu, to whom he was reluctantly obliged to submit his sketches.

After his return to Madrid in 1781, Goya received the royal invitation to paint one of seven large altarpieces for the newly built church of San Francisco el Grande in competition with Bayeu, Maella and other court painters. Goya welcomed the opportunity to further his ambition and to prove his worth by participating in this 'greatest enterprise in painting yet undertaken in Madrid'. The invitation, he wrote to his friend and chief correspondent in Saragossa, would be the means of silencing his detractors, 'those malicious people who have been so mistrustful of my merit'. Goya made several sketches for his painting, which occupied him more than a year. The result, *San Bernardino preaching*, still *in situ*, is a conventional pyramidal composition, which is today chiefly interesting for the self-portrait which he introduced among the heads of the spectators. For Goya, it represented a personal triumph as well as a stepping stone in his career. 'Certainly', he wrote to the same correspondent, Martín Zapater, 'I have been fortunate in the opinion of intelligent people and of the public at large . . . since they are all for me, without any dissentient voice. I do not yet know what result will come from above: we shall see when the King returns to Madrid.' The King's opinion must have been favourable, for, a year after the paintings were first shown to the public – that is in 1785 – Goya was appointed Deputy Director of Painting in the Academy. In 1786 his desire to be made Painter to the King was at last realized.

Goya was now launched as a fashionable court painter and entered upon the most productive and successful period of his life. 'I had established for myself an enviable way of life,' he wrote to Zapater in 1786, 'no longer dancing attendance on anyone. Those who wanted something of me sought me out. I made myself wanted more, and if it was not someone very grand or recommended by some friend I did not work for anyone, and just because I made myself so indispensable they did not (and still do not) leave me alone so that I do not know how I am to carry out everything . . .' This was no empty boast. Anyone who was anyone appears to have wanted to sit to Goya: the royal family, the aristocracy and court officials. In 1783, he painted the portrait of the chief minister of state, the Conde de Floridablanca, in which he himself appears. In the same year he painted the family portrait of the Infante Don Luis, the King's brother, with himself again in the picture, and in the following year the court architect, Ventura Rodríguez. In 1785, he was commissioned for a series of portraits of officers of the Banco Nacional de San Carlos. In these early official portraits, Goya adopted conventional 18th-century poses, and only slightly modified the polished finish of Mengs. His portraits of society ladies in outdoor settings recall contemporary English portraits as well as his own tapestry cartoons. In such portraits as that of the Marquesa de Pontejos (National Gallery, Washington), the stiff elegance of the figure and the fluent painting of the elaborate costume reflect his study of Velázquez's Infantas. His portrait of Charles III in hunting costume is based directly on Velázquez's royal huntsmen.

Among Goya's early admirers and most important patrons during a period of twenty years were the Duke and Duchess of Osuna, who not only commissioned portraits of themselves and a family group, but also a number of paintings to decorate their country residence near Madrid, the Alameda Palace, known as *El Capricho*. These paintings are similar in character to the tapestry cartoons and close in style to the sketches for them but the range of subjects is wider. In addition to the genre scenes, there are some which appear to represent actual occurrences – bandits attacking a coach, a woman fainting after falling from an ass (Pl. 6) – as well as representations of witchcraft, two of which are based on scenes from plays (Pl. 19). Among other paintings for the Duke of Osuna are two altarpieces, commissioned in 1788 for the chapel of his ancestor, S. Francisco de Borja, in Valencia Cathedral, which are more dramatic in character and in treatment than any of Goya's earlier religious compositions.

The death of Charles III in 1788, a few months before the outbreak of the French Revolution, brought to an end the period of comparative prosperity and enlightenment in Spain in which Goya had slowly reached maturity. The rule of reaction and political and social corruption that followed – stimulated by events in France – under the weak and foolish Charles IV and his clever, unscrupulous Queen María Luisa was to end in the Napoleonic invasion of Spain.

Under the new régime Goya reached the height of his career as the most fashionable and successful artist in Spain. The new King raised him to the rank of Court Painter (*Pintor de Cámara*) in 1789 and in 1792 he felt his position in the Academy assured enough to submit a report on the study of art, among other things, recommending the setting aside of the form of teaching established by Mengs, which had prevailed there. At the death of Francisco Bayeu in 1795, Goya succeeded his former teacher as Director of Painting in the Academy (but resigned for reasons of health two years later), and in 1799 he was appointed First Court Painter (*Primer Pintor de Cámara*). Goya evidently welcomed official honours and worldly success with almost naïve enthusiasm. 'The King and Queen are mad about your friend Goya', he wrote, announcing this last honour to his friend in Saragossa. Yet the record that he has left in paint of some of his patrons – including members of the royal family – is ruthlessly critical.

During a visit to Andalusia towards the end of 1792, Goya was struck down by a long and serious illness of which the effect, even a year later, made him, he wrote, 'at times rage with so ill an humour that he could not tolerate himself.' The nature of the illness is not known for certain but it caused temporary paralysis and partial blindness and left him permanently deaf, so that henceforth he could only communicate by writing or sign language. He returned to Madrid in the summer of 1793 and in the following January sent a series of eleven small paintings to Bernardo de Iriarte, Vice Protector of the Academy, with a covering letter in which he wrote: 'In order to occupy an imagination mortified by the contemplation of my sufferings and to recover part of the very great expense they have occasioned, I devoted myself to painting a group of cabinet pictures in which I have succeeded in making observations for which there is normally no opportunity in commissioned works, which give no scope for fantasy and invention.'

Of these eleven pictures of various 'national diversions' it is not possible to say much. They were shown, we know, at a meeting of members of the Academy, who expressed approval of them. Their subsequent history is not known, but there are in the Academy today five paintings which probably correspond to five of them (see Pls. 11, 13, 14). These five were not presented to the Academy in Goya's lifetime, but since the painter had asked that the pictures should be sent on to another patron after they had been seen at the Academy, this does not tell against the identification. Nor does the argument that one of the five shows an Inquisition scene and that this would have been an unlikely subject for Goya to paint while the Inquisition was still active in Spain. Such a scene was no more daring than those shown in many of the *Caprichos* which he was to publish within a few years. Stylistically, the five putative survivors of the original group represent a new departure. Their free sketchy technique with bold splashes of colour and black outline, foreshadowing Goya's later style, need not indicate a late date for them. The lack of a consistent stylistic development has already been remarked on in relation to the tapestry cartoons, and this inconsistency is present throughout Goya's works. Thus it is permissible to see these pictures as a further step in the increasing variety of his manner. His range of subject, too, was widening in all three media –

painting, drawing and engraving. From now on uncommissioned works give full scope to 'observation', 'fantasy' and 'invention'. For his commissioned works Goya continues to use conventional formulas.

In the years after his illness Goya produced some of his most sensitive and delicately painted portraits – the silvery-toned likenesses of his brother-in-law, Francisco Bayeu (Pl. 8), Andrés del Peral (Pl. 24), the intimate yet formal portrait of his friend and protector, the liberal Minister and writer, Gaspar Melchor de Jovellanos (Private Collection, Madrid), for instance. The characterization of the heads, which is so notable in these paintings, is surprisingly absent in the two delicately but stiffly painted portraits of the Duchess of Alba, of the same period. In each case the face of the Duchess, famous for her beauty, is that of a painted doll; there is no hint in the execution of the portrait of 1797 (Pl. 9), for example, of the probable intimacy between the artist and the sitter. On the contrary, it is carefully veiled: only the inscription, recently uncovered, to which she points seems to indicate the nature of the relationship. Yet at the time when he painted this portrait, during his stay at her Andalusian estate after her husband's death, Goya was recording, in a sketchbook, many lively, intimate scenes in the everyday life of the Duchess and her household.

At about this time Goya was also making drawings for a very different purpose, the series of eighty etchings published in 1799, called *Los Caprichos*. In these the artist used the popular imagery of caricature in a highly original and inventive form for his first venture in the criticism of political, social and religious abuses, for which he is famous. His mastery of the recently developed technique of aquatint makes these etchings also a major achievement in the history of engraving. Despite the veiled language of the *Caprichos* they were withdrawn from sale after a few days. Yet, in one of those apparently inexplicable contradictions in which the life of Goya abounds, when the plates and surplus copies were offered to the King in 1803, they were accepted and Goya was rewarded with a pension for his son. Many years later, Goya spoke of having nevertheless been denounced to the Inquisition – at what date and with what consequences we do not know.

What we do know is that only a few months after the publication of the *Caprichos* Goya was promoted to the rank of First Court Painter. Whether or not they were withdrawn for political reasons, Goya's success and official position with his royal patrons appears to have been unaffected at the time either by the *Caprichos* or by his increasingly unconventional treatment of conventional subjects. His fresco decorations in the Church of San Antonio de la Florida, a royal commission executed in 1798, in the space of a few months (Pls. 16 and 20), owe very little to earlier religious frescoes. The over life-size figures are painted in a broad free style, in strong colours, with hardly any detail, that has no precedent in Goya's oeuvre (unless the much smaller 'popular diversions' in the Academy were painted during his convalescence in 1793). Though Goya in this same period was painting religious subjects such as the *St. Gregory* (Pl. 5), and the *Taking of Christ* in the Sacristy of Toledo Cathedral (1798) in conventional terms, here he has concentrated on the overall decorative effect. The *Miracle of St. Anthony*, the central theme, is almost overshadowed by the surrounding populace and by the angels in the shape of women below.

Even less conventional than the San Antonio frescoes are Goya's portraits of his royal patrons. From the time of their accession until 1800, Charles IV and María Luisa sat to him on many occasions, and many replicas were made of his portraits. He painted them in various costumes and poses, ranging from the early decorative portraits in full regalia in the earlier tradition of Mengs to the simpler and more natural compositions in the manner of Velázquez, who directly inspired the large equestrian portraits in the Prado Museum. But while following traditional compositions for these state portraits, Goya creates an effect of pomposity rather than majesty and the faces of his sitters reveal a penetrating scrutiny of character. Nowhere is this more striking than in the portrait of *Charles IV and his Family* (painted in 1800: Pls. 15 and 17). Though Goya doubtless had in mind Velázquez's unique royal portrait group, *Las Meninas*, which he had copied in an engraving years before, his royal assembly lacks any semblance of courtly dignity and elegance. Moreover, despite the official character of the painting and his official position, he has accentuated the ugliness and vulgarity of the principal figures so vividly as to produce an effect almost of caricature. Théophile Gautier, writing of this picture, remarks that the King 'looks like a grocer who has just won the lottery prize, with his family around him'.

Goya as First Court Painter seems to have been more ready than ever to express an opinion of his sitters in his portraits of them. The portrait of the Countess of Chinchón (1800), for example, is a sympathetic portrayal of the young pregnant wife of Manuel Godoy, 'Prince of the Peace' and Chief Minister, the lover of Queen María Luisa. Godoy's own portrait (1801) is a somewhat theatrical composition, which may hint at the disrespect that was almost certainly intended in several plates of the *Caprichos*. Godoy was, nevertheless, an important patron of the artist. His palace was decorated with allegorical paintings by Goya, he not only sat to him on more than one occasion for his portrait but had his wife painted by him and he owned versions of Goya's portraits of the King and Queen. It is, moreover, in Godoy's collection that the *Maja desnuda* (Pl. 22) and the *Maja vestida* (Pl. 23) are first recorded, and the importance of his position makes it possible that they were painted for him. The possibility is strengthened by his known taste – he owned among other such pictures Velázquez's 'Rokeby Venus' – but it cannot be asserted that he actually commissioned Goya's only painting of a female nude. Both the origin of the *Majas* and the identity of the model are still a mystery. Goya was summoned by the Inquisition in 1815 to explain when and for whom they had been executed, but his explanation has never been discovered.

At about the same time when the *Majas* were probably painted, i.e. before 1803, Goya seems to have suffered a loss of royal favour. The group portrait is the last occasion on which he painted either Charles IV or María Luisa, and in 1804 he was unsuccessful in his application to be made Director General of the Academy. The decline in favour has never been satisfactorily explained, though a variety of reasons have been advanced for it. Among these are the notoriety of the *Caprichos* (Goya's gift of the plates to the King in 1803 is thought by some to have been an attempt to protect himself); Goya's political sympathies (his protector Jovellanos was imprisoned in 1801); his liaison with the Duchess of Alba and the circumstances of her death in 1802; the change of taste exemplified in the appointment of Vicente López as Court Painter in 1802. The true cause may well be a royal preference for López's more flattering, neo-classical style of portraiture.

Despite his loss of official patronage, the years preceding the French invasion were for Goya prosperous and fruitful. He was rich enough to purchase a second house which he gave to his son, Francisco Javier, the only surviving child of several – though not of the legendary twenty – on his marriage in 1805. Goya's production consisted chiefly of portraits but these were of a wider range of sitters than hitherto: his son and daughter-in-law, men and women whose names are known today only because he painted them, others whose names have been forgotten, as well as some members of the court and aristocracy. In 1805, perhaps a few years after the *Majas*, he painted in a similar pose the Marquesa de Santa Cruz, daughter of his earlier patrons, the Duke and Duchess of Osuna, a young woman said to have had a taste for the unconventional. But though she is more lightly clothed than the clothed *Maja*, her attributes of wreath and lyre and the more polished style of the painting produce a more formal effect. Goya's uncommissioned works of this period include two paintings of *Majas on a balcony*, recorded in the artist's possession in 1812.

Goya was sixty-two years old when the old régime in Spain finally collapsed, with the aid of Napoleon, and Spain was subjected to six years of war and revolution. The rapidity and confusion of the events of 1808, when the French crossed the frontier, are, as it were, reflected in the history of the equestrian portrait of Ferdinand VII (Madrid, Academy of San Fernando). Goya was ordered to paint this portrait in March, after the rising at Aranjuez, which had forced the resignation of Godoy and the abdication of Charles IV. Only three sittings of three-quarters of an hour were allowed him and the picture was not exhibited until October of that year. In the meantime Napoleon had forced Ferdinand from the throne in favour of his own brother Joseph and the French had entered and been temporarily expelled from Madrid.

Goya's conduct and his continued practice in his profession during the war were in some ways equivocal but in this he was no different from many of his fellow-countrymen and friends. He was in Madrid during the tragic events of the 2nd and 3rd May when the populace rose against the French and the rising was savagely repressed – events which he later recorded in two of the most famous of his paintings (Pls. 30 and 31). After the temporary liberation of the capital he was summoned by General Palafox to Saragossa, his home town, which had recently been under siege, to inspect the ruins and record the glorious deeds of its inhabitants. He is next heard of in Madrid towards the end of 1808, when the French were again in occupation, and with thousands of other heads of families Goya swore allegiance to the French King. He also seems to have resumed his activities as Court Painter and was awarded Joseph's decoration, the Royal Order of Spain, in March 1811. Goya was one of three academicians ordered by Joseph to select fifty Spanish pictures from palaces and churches for the Musée Napoléon in Paris and seems to have done so only after long delay. When the pictures reached Paris it was reported that at the most six were worthy to enter the Museum. During the French occupation Goya painted the *Allegory of the City of Madrid* (Pl. 32), with a portrait of Joseph which he copied from an engraving. There is no record of Joseph's sitting to Goya, though several French generals and pro-French Spaniards did so. As soon as Wellington entered Madrid in 1812, Goya accepted a commission for an equestrian portrait of the liberator and, probably soon afterwards, painted two other portraits of his only recorded English sitter (Pl. 29). During the war he was also occupied with family portraits and portraits of private citizens. His uncommissioned works of the period include many paintings of the hostilities themselves and one symbolic picture, the fearful and enigmatic *Colossus* (Pl. 27). But the most moving and eloquent record that he made of the war and of his personal reactions to it are the *Desastres de la Guerra*, a series of eighty-two etchings for which he made drawings at the time, though they were not published until 1863. If at any time Goya had looked upon the French as liberators, the *Desastres* express his fierce hatred of the effects and consequences of war, just as other drawings of the period bear witness to a more generalized but no less fervent abhorrence of injustice, oppression and hypocrisy.

At the end of the war Goya and other Spaniards who had served the French King were subjected to 'purification'. Goya defended himself by claiming that he had never worn Joseph's decoration and that it had only compromised him, several witnesses supporting this statement. His defence was accepted and Goya resumed his office as First Court Painter on the restoration of Ferdinand VII. Even before the King's return, he had applied to the Regency for permission to commemorate the incidents of the 2nd and 3rd May (Pls. 30 and 31). Soon afterwards he was commissioned to paint several portraits of the King for ministries and other public buildings. For these, Goya seems to have used the same study of the head, changing only pose, setting and costume to suit the occasion. The portraits (see Pl. 33) are remarkable for a characterization that comes even closer to caricature than the portraits of María Luisa: their pompous attitudes and subtly exaggerated facial expression evoke the cruel, despotic character of the *rey deseado*, whose restoration to the throne inaugurated a new era of fanaticism and oppression. The portraits of Ferdinand were Goya's last royal portraits, apart from the appearance of the King in the *Royal Company of the Philippines* (Musée Goya, Castres). Goya was again out of favour. Whether or not his image of the King was felt to be objectionable, Ferdinand clearly preferred the more pleasing style of Vicente López for portraits of himself and family.

It may be too that Goya's liberal sympathies did not recommend him at Court. Ferdinand's reactionary measures immediately after his restoration, his repudiation of the Constitution of 1812, the re-establishment of the Inquisition, the closing of universities and theatres, the introduction of press censorship and the persecution of the liberals, including many of Goya's friends, must certainly have antagonized the artist. Although he was exonerated from the charge of having 'accepted employment from the usurper' in April 1815, in the following month he was summoned to appear before the Inquisition on account of the *Majas*. Nevertheless, Goya retained his position as First Court Painter for another decade.

Apart from the publication, in 1816, of the *Tauromaquia*, a series of etchings of the national sport of bullfighting, Goya from now on was chiefly occupied with paintings for private patrons, for friends and for himself. He also continued to record in the more intimate medium of drawing his observations and ideas. Freed from official restrictions, his style became more and more personal and his technique increasingly free and impressionistic as in the *Woman reading a letter* (Pl. 38) and the *Forge* (Pl. 39). A similar development is visible in the gradually changing style of the portraits he painted at this time. The poses, except in the case of a few official sitters, become less formal and Goya develops his technique of creating a remarkable effect of likeness by means of a minimum of detail. Pose and technique are strikingly illustrated in the self-portrait with his doctor painted in 1820 to commemorate his recovery from serious illness the year before (Minneapolis). Goya is supported in the arms of the physician, the melancholy expression that he had worn in the self-portrait of 1815 (Pl. 36) now deepened and transmuted by suffering.

It is perhaps surprising that during this period of semi-retirement Goya should have received two important ecclesiastical commissions, for the *St. Justa and St. Rufina*, painted in 1817 for Seville Cathedral, and for the *Last Communion of St. Joseph of Calasanz*, which he painted in 1819 for the church of the Escuelas Pías de San Antón in Madrid. In these he adapted his late style to traditional subject matter and turned to seventeenth-century Spanish painting for his models. While the Seville picture has been criticized for its profane character, the *Last Communion* is more suggestive of religious devotion than any of Goya's earlier religious works.

No hint of anything so conventional is apparent in the famous 'black paintings' now in the Prado (Pls. 42–45), the terrifying images with which he decorated his house on the outskirts of Madrid, the *Quinta del Sordo*. These paintings must have been executed between 1820, after his illness, and 1823 when Goya made over the *Quinta* to his grandson. Their entirely new, expressionist language and grim fantasy make them, along with the *Proverbios* or *Disparates* (a series of etchings made about the same time, though not published until 1864) the most private and tortuous of all his works. Their subjects, sinister, horrific and mysterious, and their atmosphere of nightmare seem the product of cynicism, pessimism and despair. Paradoxically, the period of their painting corresponded to a liberal interlude, forced upon Ferdinand by widespread revolt, but lasting only three years. When the French army restored the King to absolute power in 1823, the persecution of the liberals was renewed with greater violence than ever before. Goya, who had made his last appearance at the Academy on 4 April, 1820 to swear allegiance to the Constitution, went into hiding early in 1824. Many of his friends had already left the country or were in similar concealment. After the declaration of amnesty of that year, he applied for in May – and was granted – leave of absence to travel to France, allegedly to take the waters at Plombières for his health. He went first to Bordeaux, where several of his friends had settled, arriving there in June, according to one of them 'deaf, old, slow and feeble – and so happy and so eager to see the world'. From Bordeaux he went on to Paris, where he spent two months in the company of Spanish refugees, leaving the house, according to the police record 'only to see the sights of the city and to roam the streets'. Back in Bordeaux, Goya set up house with Leocadia Weiss, who had come from Spain with her two children, for the younger of whom he is known to have had a special affection. He taught her to draw and had great, but unfulfilled, hopes of her talent.

Goya remained in Bordeaux for the rest of his life, except for two short visits to Madrid in 1826 and 1827. On the former he offered his resignation as First Court Painter and was pensioned off. 'I am eighty years old', he wrote to the King, 'I have served your august parents and grandfather for fifty-three years.' During the visit he sat to Vicente López, his successor.

Until the end of his life Goya, in spite of old age and infirmity, continued to record the world around him in paintings and drawings and in the new technique of lithography which he had already begun to use before leaving Spain. 'Sight and pulse, pen and inkwell, everything fails me and only my will is to spare', he wrote to his old friend Joaquín Ferrer in Paris in December 1825. But even now he was turning to something new. In the same letter, evidently a reply to a suggestion that the *Caprichos* would be saleable in Paris, he announced that he had 'better things today which could be sold to greater effect. To be sure', he continued, 'last winter I painted on ivory a collection of nearly forty examples, but it is original miniature painting such as I have never seen for it is not done with stippling and they look more like the brushwork of Velázquez than of Mengs.' A number of these miniatures have survived and are indeed original in subject matter, style and technique. Instead of the usual portraits, Goya shows such subjects as a young woman, half-naked, leaning on a rock (Boston), a monk and an old woman, a *majo* and *maja* (Stockholm). Instead of the careful finish usual in miniatures, we have the broad sketchy style of Goya's last years. His technique, so different from that of the conventional miniaturist, is described by Matheron, whose information about Goya's years in Bordeaux is based on the first-hand evidence of the artist's companion and compatriot, Antonio Brugada: 'He blackened the ivory plaque and let fall on it a drop of water which, as it spread, lifted off part of the black ground and traced chance lines. Goya made use of these furrows and always brought out something original and unexpected. These little productions belong to the same family as the *Caprichos*.'

During these last years in Bordeaux, Goya painted a number of still-life subjects (Pl. 47), observed, according to Matheron, in the market-place and executed on his return home, 'in a hand's turn, between two cigarettes'. A few genre subjects and some portraits of his friends complete the catalogue of his paintings. The genre scenes of the year before Goya's death – the *Milkmaid of Bordeaux*, the *Head of a Monk* and the *Head of a Nun* – are difficult to categorize. Like many of his earlier uncommissioned works, they seem to belong neither to genre proper, nor to religious painting, nor to portraiture. The portraits of Santiago Galos (1826, Barnes Collection, Philadelphia), Juan de Muguiro (1827, Prado), José Pío de Molina (1828, Reinhardt Collection, Winterthur) are the most remarkable illustrations of the final development of his style. 'There again,' writes Matheron, who had seen weakness of touch and uncertainty of drawing in the still-life and other late paintings, 'before the living model, a double *binocle* on his nose, he found himself again for a brief space.'

The free handling of form and colour in these last paintings, the assurance with which they achieve their effect in terms of light and shade, without outline or detail and in a narrow range of tones, make them today among the most admired of Goya's works. Nearly forty years before he painted them, in 1792, Goya had announced his credo: 'There are no rules in painting. . . . Even those who have gone furthest in the matter can give few rules about the deep play of understanding that is needed, or say how it came about that they were sometimes more successful in a work executed with less care than in one on which they had spent most time. What a profound and impenetrable mystery is locked up in the imitation of divine nature, without which there is nothing good. . . .' In his old age, Matheron reports, he mocked the academicians and their methods of teaching: 'Always lines, never forms', he is reported to have said in one of his rare conversations about painting. 'But where do they find these lines in nature? Personally I only see forms that are lit up and forms that are not, planes which advance and planes which recede, relief and depth. My eye never sees outlines or particular features or details. I do not count the hairs in the beard of the man who passes by any more than the buttonholes on his jacket attract my notice. My brush should not see better than I do.' And again: 'In nature, colour does not exist any more than lines. There is only light and shadow. Give me a piece of charcoal and I will make you a picture. All painting is a matter of sacrifice and *parti-pris*.' The reduction of Goya's palette had come slowly and step by step with his abandonment of academic style. The brightly coloured and decorative tapestry cartoons, with which his career was launched, belong to another world and an earlier century. It is the works of his maturity and old age, varied, penetrating, sombre, melancholy, violent, technically audacious, which made Goya's reputation as the greatest master of his age and the first of the moderns. Our last records of Goya's life are letters to his son in which he expresses his joy at the prospect of a visit from his grandson and daughter-in-law and his impatience to see them. They arrived on 28 March, shortly before Goya wrote his last lines to his son: 'I can only say that such joy has made me a little indisposed and I am in bed.' A few days later he suffered a paralytic stroke and died on 16 April, 1828.

1746 Born on 30 March at Fuendetodos, Aragon, the son of José Goya, a master gilder. About 1760 he goes to live in Saragossa, where he studies art for four years with José Luzán.

1763 and 1766 Competes unsuccessfully for scholarships offered by the Royal Academy of San Fernando, Madrid. At this time he probably works in the studio of the Aragonese painter, Francisco Bayeu, in Madrid. About 1769/70 he goes to Italy, at his own expense.

1771 April: from Rome he submits a painting to a competition held by the Academy in Parma which wins honourable mention. Later in the year, back in Saragossa, he receives his first official commission for frescoes in the Cathedral of El Pilar, in collaboration with Francisco Bayeu.

1773 25 July: marries Josefa Bayeu, sister of Francisco and Ramón Bayeu, in Madrid.

1774 Invited by the Court Painter Anton Raphael Mengs to paint cartoons for tapestries woven by the Royal Factory of Santa Barbara, work that occupies him intermittently until 1792.

1780 With his painting of the *Crucifixion* (Prado), Goya is unanimously elected to membership of the Academy of San Fernando. He returns to Saragossa to paint further frescoes in El Pilar.

1781 Back in Madrid, he receives a royal invitation to paint one of seven altarpieces for the new Church of San Francisco el Grande.

1784 2 December: birth of his son Francisco Javier, the only child of several to survive infancy (d. 1854).

1785 Appointed Deputy Director of Painting in the Academy of San Fernando.

1786 Appointed Painter to the King, Charles III.

1789 Raised to the rank of Court Painter by Charles IV, who had succeeded to the throne in the previous year.

1792 14 October: submits a report on the study of art to the Academy.

1792-3 During a visit to his friend Sebastian Martínez in Cadiz, Goya suffers a serious illness which leaves him permanently deaf. On recovering he paints a series of uncommissioned cabinet pictures which he submits to the Vice Protector of the Academy in January 1794.

1795 On the death of Francisco Bayeu, Goya succeeds him as Director of Painting in the Academy but resigns two years later for reasons of health.

1797 Visits the recently widowed Duchess of Alba at her Andalusian estate, Sanlúcar de Barrameda.

1799 February: announcement of the publication of the *Caprichos*, which are shortly afterwards withdrawn from sale. October: appointed First Court Painter.

1802 Death of the Duchess of Alba.

1803 Offers the plates and unsold copies of the *Caprichos* to the King, who accepts them and rewards him with a pension for his son.

1804 Applies unsuccessfully for the post of Director General of the Academy.

1805 His son Francisco Javier marries Gumersinda Goicoechea.

1806 10 July: birth of his grandson Mariano (d. 1874).

1808 In Madrid at the time of the French invasion and the popular rising of 2 May; then summoned by General Palafox to Saragossa to record the events of the recent siege. After his return to Madrid, in December he takes an oath of allegiance to the French King Joseph Bonaparte.

1811 Awarded the Royal Order of Spain by Joseph Bonaparte.

1811 3 June: Goya and his wife make their wills.

1812 20 June: death of his wife. According to an inventory of their possessions dated 28 October, a number of his paintings are assigned to his son, Francisco Javier.

1814 After the expulsion of the French from Spain, Goya is among those accused of having collaborated and is exonerated in April 1815. On the return of Ferdinand VII, he resumes his office as First Court Painter.

1815 May: summoned to appear before the Inquisition to account for his paintings of the *Majas*.

1817 Journey to Seville in connection with a commission for the painting of *St. Justa and St. Rufina* for the Cathedral.

1819 27 February: buys the *Quinta del Sordo*, a house on the outskirts of Madrid, where he lives until 1823/4.

1820 4 April: makes his last appearance at the Academy at a special session to swear allegiance to the recently restored liberal Constitution of 1812.

1823 17 September: makes a gift of the *Quinta del Sordo* to his grandson Mariano.

1824 At the threat of renewed political persecutions, Goya goes into hiding with an Aragonese friend and, after an amnesty, on 2 May he applies for permission to go to France to take the waters at Plombières. After two months in Paris, he settles in September in Bordeaux, where he is joined by Leocadia Weiss and her two children, with whom he sets up house.

1826 Makes a brief visit to Madrid, resigns as Court Painter and is given leave to return to France.

1828 16 April: dies, a few days after the arrival of his grandson and daughter-in-law, at Bordeaux, where he is buried. In 1901 his remains (with the head missing) are taken to Spain to be re-interred in 1919 in the Church of San Antonio de la Florida, Madrid, which he had decorated with frescoes in 1798.

List of plates

1. *Boys blowing up a Balloon.* Canvas, 116 × 124 cm. 1777–8. Madrid, Prado.

2. *Boys playing at Soldiers.* Canvas, 29 × 42 cm. About 1776–86. Glasgow, Pollok House, Stirling Maxwell Collection.

3. *The Snowstorm.* Canvas, 275 × 293 cm. 1786–7. Madrid, Prado.

4. *The Injured Mason.* Canvas, 268 × 110 cm. 1786–7. Madrid, Prado.

5. *St. Gregory.* Canvas, 188 × 113 cm. About 1797. Madrid, Museo Romántico.

6. *La Caída* (The Fall). Canvas, 169 × 100 cm. 1786–7. Madrid, Duque de Montellano.

7. *La Cucaña* (The Greasy Pole). Canvas, 169 × 88 cm. 1786–7. Madrid, Duque de Montellano.

8. *Portrait of Francisco Bayeu.* Canvas, 112 × 84 cm. About 1795. Madrid, Prado.

9. *Portrait of the Duchess of Alba.* Canvas, 210 × 148 cm. 1797. New York, The Hispanic Society of America.

10. *El Pelele* (The Straw Manikin). Canvas, 267 × 160 cm. 1791–2. Madrid, Prado.

11. *The Burial of the Sardine.* Panel, 82 × 60 cm. 1793(?). Madrid, Academy of San Fernando.

12. *Blind Man's Buff.* Canvas, 269 × 350 cm. 1789. Madrid, Prado.

13. *A Village Bullfight.* Panel, 45 × 72 cm. 1793(?). Madrid, Academy of San Fernando.

14. *The Madhouse.* Panel, 45 × 72 cm. 1793(?). Madrid, Academy of San Fernando.

15. *Charles IV and his Family.* Canvas, 280 × 336 cm. 1800. Madrid, Prado.

16. *Detail of the Crowd witnessing the Miracle of St. Anthony.* Detail of the decoration of the cupola of the church of San Antonio de la Florida, Madrid. Fresco. 1798.

17. *Queen María Luisa:* detail of plate 15.

18. *A Picnic.* Canvas, 41·3 × 25·8 cm. 1788(?). London, National Gallery.

19. *The Bewitched Man.* Canvas, 42·5 × 30·8 cm. About 1798. London, National Gallery.

20. *Detail of the Crowd witnessing the Miracle of St. Anthony.* Detail of the decoration of the cupola of the church of San Antonio de la Florida, Madrid. Fresco. 1798.

21. *Portrait of the Infante Don Francisco de Paula Antonio.* Canvas, 74 × 60 cm. 1800. Madrid, Prado.

22. *La Maja Desnuda* (The Naked Maja). Canvas, 97 × 190 cm. About 1800–3. Madrid, Prado.

23. *La Maja Vestida* (The Clothed Maja). Canvas, 95 × 190 cm. About 1800–3. Madrid, Prado.

24. *Portrait of Andrés del Peral.* Panel, 95 × 65·7 cm. 1798. London, National Gallery.

25. *Portrait of Antonia Zárate.* Canvas, 103·5 × 81·9 cm. About 1805. Blessington, Ireland, Sir Alfred Beit, Bt.

26. *Portrait of Victor Guye.* 104·5 × 83·5 cm. 1810. Washington, D.C., The National Gallery of Art.

27. *The Colossus.* Canvas, 116 × 105 cm. About 1810–12. Madrid, Prado.

28. *Portrait of Francisca Sabasa García.* 71 × 58 cm. About 1806–8. Washington, D.C., The National Gallery of Art (Mellon Collection).

29. *Portrait of the Duke of Wellington.* Panel, 64 × 52 cm. 1812. London, National Gallery.

30. *The 2nd of May, 1808: The Charge of the Mamelukes.* 266 × 345 cm. 1814. Madrid, Prado.

31. *The 3rd of May, 1808: The Execution of the Defenders of Madrid.* Canvas, 266 × 345 cm. 1814. Madrid, Prado.

32. *Allegory of the City of Madrid.* Canvas, 260 × 195 cm. 1810. Madrid, Ayuntamiento.

33. *Portrait of Ferdinand VII.* Canvas, 207 × 144 cm. About 1814. Madrid, Prado.

34. Detail of plate 31.

35. *A Prison Scene.* Zinc, 42·9 × 31·7 cm. About 1810–14. Barnard Castle, Bowes Museum.

36. *Self-portrait.* Canvas, 46 × 35 cm. About 1815. Madrid, Prado.

37. *Portrait of Mariano Goya, the Artist's Grandson.* Panel, 59 × 47 cm. About 1812–14. Madrid, Duque de Albuquerque.

38. *A Woman reading a Letter.* Canvas, 181 × 122 cm. About 1814–18. Lille, Musée des Beaux-Arts.

39. *The Forge.* Canvas, 191 × 121 cm. About 1819. New York, The Frick Collection.

40. *Portrait of Juan Antonio Cuervo.* Canvas, 120 × 87 cm. 1819. Cleveland, Museum of Art.

41. *Portrait of Ramón Satué.* Canvas, 104 × 81·3 cm. 1823(?). Amsterdam, Rijksmuseum.

42. *Fantastic Vision* (detail). Canvas (whole painting), 123 × 265 cm. About 1820–3. Madrid, Prado.

43. *Pilgrimage to San Isidro* (detail). Canvas (whole painting), 140 × 438 cm. About 1820–3. Madrid, Prado.

44. *Laughing Figures.* Canvas, 125 × 66 cm. About 1820–3. Madrid, Prado.

45. *Saturn devouring one of his Children.* Canvas, 146 × 83 cm. About 1820–3. Madrid, Prado.

46. *Tío Paquete.* Canvas, 39·1 × 31·1 cm. About 1820. Lugano, Thyssen Collection.

47. *Still Life: A Butcher's Counter.* Canvas, 45 × 62 cm. About 1824. Paris, Louvre.

48. *St. Peter Repentant.* Canvas, 29 × 25½ cm. About 1823–5. Washington, D.C., The Phillips Collection.

1. **Boys blowing up a Balloon.** 1777-1778. Madrid, Prado

2. **Boys playing at Soldiers.** About 1776-1786. Glasgow, Pollok House, Stirling Maxwell Collection

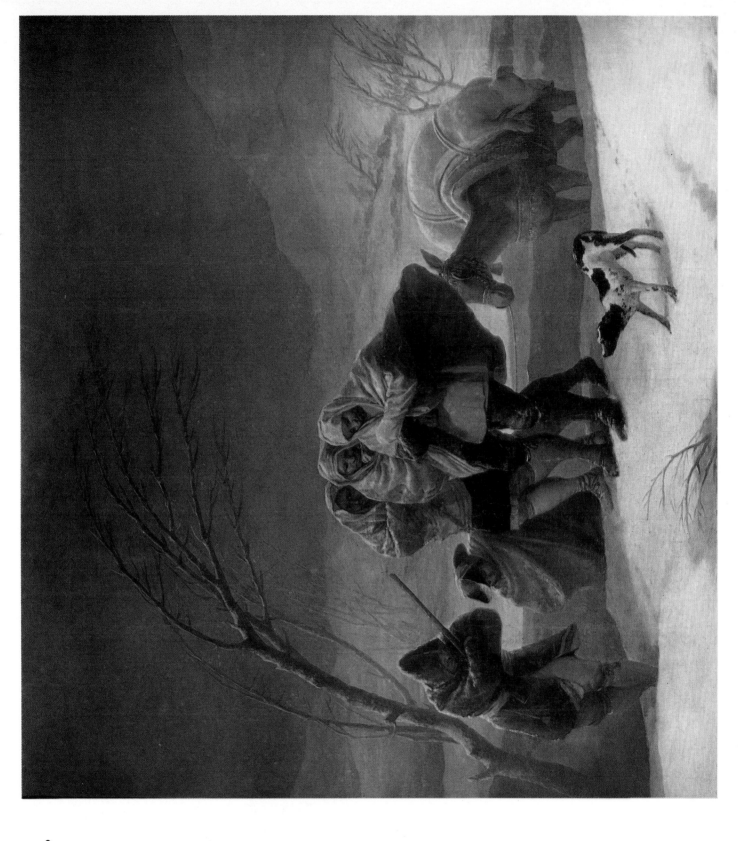

3. **The Snowstorm.**
1786-1787. Madrid, Prado

4. The Injured Mason. 1786-1787. Madrid, Prado

5. **St. Gregory.** About 1797. Madrid, Museo Romántico

6. **La Caída (The Fall).** 1786-1787. Madrid, Duque de Montellano

7. **La Cucaña (The Greasy Pole).** 1786-1787. Madrid, Duque de Montellano

8. **Portrait of Francisco Bayeu.** About 1795. Madrid, Prado

9. **Portrait of the Duchess of Alba.** 1797. New York, The Hispanic Society of America

10. **El Pelele (The Straw Manikin).** 1791-1792. Madrid, Prado

11. **The Burial of the Sardine.** 1793(?). Madrid, Academy of San Fernando

12. **Blind Man's Buff.** 1789. Madrid, Prado

13. **A Village Bullfight.** 1793(?). Madrid, Academy of San Fernando

14. **The Madhouse.** 1793(?). Madrid, Academy of San Fernando

16. **Detail of the Crowd witnessing the Miracle of St. Anthony.** 1798. Madrid, San Antonio de la Florida

17. **Queen María Luisa** (detail of Plate 15)

18. **A Picnic.** 1788(?). London, National Gallery

19. **The Bewitched Man.** About 1798. London, National Gallery

20. **Detail of the Crowd witnessing the Miracle of St. Anthony.** 1798. Madrid, San Antonio de la Florida

21. **Portrait of the Infante don Francisco de Paula Antonio.** 1800. Madrid, Prado

22. **La Maja Desnuda (The Naked Maja).** About 1800-1803. Madrid, Prado

23. **La Maja Vestida (The Clothed Maja).** About 1800-1803. Madrid, Prado

24.   **Portrait of Andrés del Peral.** 1798. London, National Gallery

25. **Portrait of Antonia Zárate.** About 1805. Blessington, Ireland, Sir Alfred Beit, Bt.

26. **Portrait of Victor Guye.** 1810. Washington, D.C., National Gallery of Art

27.   **The Colossus.** About 1810-1812. Madrid, Prado

28. **Portrait of Francisca Sabasa García.** About 1806-1808. Washington, D.C., National Gallery of Art (Mellon Collection)

29. **Portrait of the Duke of Wellington.** 1812. London, National Gallery

Execution of the Defenders of Madrid. 1814. Madrid, Prado

32. **Allegory of the City of Madrid.** 1810. Madrid, Ayuntamiento

33. **Portrait of Ferdinand VII.** About 1814. Madrid, Prado

34. Detail of Plate 31

35. **A Prison Scene.** About 1810-1814. Barnard Castle, County Durham, Bowes Museum

36. **Self-portrait.** About 1815. Madrid, **Prado**

37. **Portrait of Mariano Goya, the Artist's Grandson.** About 1812-1814. Madrid, Duque de Albuquerque

38. **A Woman reading a Letter.** About 1814-1818. Lille, Musée des Beaux-Arts

39. **The Forge.** About 1819. New York, The Frick Collection

40. Portrait of Juan Antonio Cuervo. 1819. Cleveland, Museum of Art

41. **Portrait of Ramón Satué**. 1823(?). Amsterdam, Rijksmuseum

42. **Fantastic Vision** (detail). About 1820-1823. Madrid, Prado

43. **Pilgrimage to San Isidro** (detail). About 1820-1823. Madrid, Prado

44. **Laughing Figures.** About 1820-1823. Madrid, Prado

45. **Saturn devouring one of his Children.** About 1820-1823. Madrid. Prado

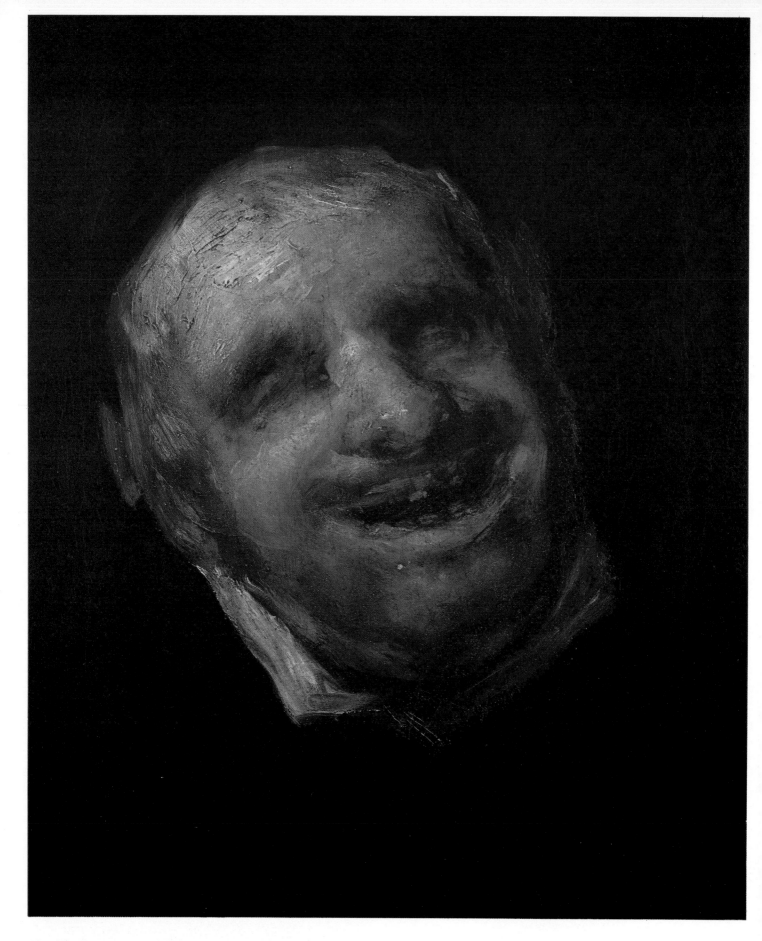

46. **Tío Paquete.** About 1820. Lugano, Thyssen Collection

47.   **Still Life: A Butcher's Counter.** About 1824. Paris, Louvre

48. **St. Peter Repentant.** About 1823-1825. Washington, D.C., The Phillips Collection

07. APR 09

C014449737